COMPASSIONATE SUCCESS

The Leadership Guide to *Accelerate* and *Maximize* Organizational Growth

Kymberli S.J. Speight

CERTIFIED

(H)

WRITTEN
BY HUMAN

COMPASSIONATE
SUCCESS

CONTENTS

PREFACE

For over two decades, Kymberli S. Speight has held leadership roles, delivered more than 400 presentations, and coached and consulted senior executives across industries. In this inspiring book, she introduces fresh perspectives on a familiar truth — that momentum-building relationships are the cornerstone of both personal and professional success.

With candor, insight, and humor, Kymberli invites readers to explore the transformative power of connection. Each chapter begins with a personal reflection. There is also a free self-assessment to help you uncover thoughts that may be holding you back from your goals. In addition, there is an Others Focused vs. Me Focused "3-Score" Challenge to personally test whether you have a healthy balance between your wants and others.

As you journey through these pages, you'll gain practical tools and renewed clarity to strengthen your leadership, elevate your teams, and rediscover what truly drives sustained success: relationships built with compassion, authenticity, and purpose.

If you ever spot Kymberli in an airport, you'll know it's her — wearing her favorite travel jacket, embroidered with the words that define her life's work: "Connections Matter."

FOREWORD

In times of turmoil, vacillating priorities, and vast differences among segments of our society, what could be more comforting than a book dedicated to reinforcing the importance of building, leveraging, and expanding relationships that drive organizational and personal success?

Based upon her decades of experience and the insights she has developed, Kymberli Speight offers seasoned leaders, transitioning leaders, and those aspiring to higher leadership roles a unique perspective on the criticality of developing soft skills that lead to increased engagement, clarity of organizational vision, bottom-line success, and mission accomplishment.

Her insights provide readers with a clear understanding of what it takes to overcome challenges and achieve success that is long-lasting and has the potential to exceed expectations.

Kym has captured the essence of the mindset and behaviors leaders need to thrive and excel in the future.

— Carl Bryant, PhD, Lt Col (Ret.), USAF
Former Senior Partner, Korn Ferry International (2013-2014)
Former Vice President, Center for Creative Leadership (1993-2004)

ENDORSEMENTS

What a fantastic read! Kymberli Speight gets "it" and lives out her life with "Compassionate Success."

This book is a must-read for people in positions of leadership and those striving to get there. In fact, this is a must-read for people in all stages of life looking for contentment through authentic relationships and the success that follows. Kymberli lays out the process within each chapter with precision and steps to not only maximize growth, but also the type of organizational development where all feel a great sense of satisfaction. Each chapter provides keys toward this end by pushing forward strategic steps to intentionally impact those whom one may meet along the way.

Don't miss out! The time you spend reading through this *Leadership Guide to Accelerate and Maximize Organizational Growth* will provide long-term benefits for life, along with a great ROI from the time spent to digest its content. Kymberli has carefully prepared steps and tools for authentic growth and has knocked it out of the park! I remain truly grateful for the compassionate impact she has had on my life.

Jeff A. Walker,
Owner, Walker Investments & Chadwicks Fitness
Owner and Chairman, Ellsworth Systems

Compassionate Success is a practical and inspiring roadmap for leaders who want to build a people-focused organization. Kymberli's insights on relational capital resonated with me as a 27-year CEO and provided a clear path with actionable steps to transform culture, strengthen teams, and achieve organizational success in today's evolving workspace.

Glenn L. Strebe
CEO Air Academy Credit Union

Kymberli Speight's book is a practical and helpful guide for both new and incumbent leaders. It provides simple, actionable steps to help leaders and organizations reach their potential — while always keeping in mind the most important precept — it's about the people. It is an enjoyable, easy read. You will come away as a better leader by following her principles.

Ezra Singer
CEO Ezra Singer + Associates
Former CHRO Verizon

The only LASTING success is "Compassionate Success!" In this powerful new book, Kymberli Speight provides a clear, simple, and compelling GPS to the ultimate destination for leaders... impact through people-focused and compassionate energy! In a world enamored with AI, Kymberli helps us remember that we are all in the PEOPLE business, first and foremost. She skillfully shows us how to build teams and relationships in challenging times. You'll discover countless pearls of insight that will elevate your positive influence on everyone you touch!

Brian Biro
Speaker, author
America's Breakthrough Speaker

INTRODUCTION

On a day thick with tension, Austin Department of Public Safety officers were stationed at the Central Services Building while news crews lingered outside. Inside, locksmiths were at the ready.

That morning, the Texas Facilities Commission (TFC) board voted 5-2 to remove its executive director. A Texas Tribune investigation had exposed what many already suspected – the agency was paralyzed by dysfunction. Years of poor leadership had left the agency broken – with outdated policies, disengaged employees, and a toxic culture. The Commission managed billions of taxpayer dollars, yet basic tools like an organizational chart didn't exist. People were jockeying for power instead of solving problems.

Within 24 hours of that meeting, seven more TFC executives either resigned or were shown the door. The Commission lost nearly its entire top tier: the CFO, general counsel, HR director, and operations chief.

If you're a college football fan, the best comparison is the NCAA's "death penalty" issued to Southern Methodist University in 1987 for repeated and flagrant recruiting violations. It took SMU years to recover from that scandal.

But unlike SMU, the TFC couldn't cancel its season. Its mission – building and maintaining state facilities – was far too important. The work had to continue.

This was the agency Mike Novak, already one of the TFC's board members, walked into as its new leader. The challenges facing the agency were immense: stalled projects, deferred maintenance, shell-shocked employees, and skeptical lawmakers. The easy path would have been to manage appearances, patch holes, and hope people forgot the crisis.

Some leaders in that situation might have tried to bulldoze their way through the problems. Quite a few published works by the American Management Association, Deloitte, the National College of Ireland, and the University of Pretoria cite common mistakes by leaders in organizational turnarounds that include acting too quickly without proper diagnosis, overlooking organizational culture, avoiding difficult conversations, poor communication, lack of alignment among leadership, and treating transformation as a short-term project, but Novak chose a different route. He started by listening. On his first day, he gathered the remaining executives and asked them to email him three to five things that kept them up at night. He wasn't looking for a quick fix; he simply wanted to understand the situation.

What he discovered confirmed what he already suspected: the culture was toxic, and the people were tired. Instead of treating his executives like disposable parts, Novak treated them as people. He asked questions. He cared enough to understand not just what they were doing, but what they were afraid of.

And that care made him relatable. Whether he was talking with lawmakers, employees, or ranchers along the border, Novak knew success depended on understanding their mindsets.

CEOs, presidents, and senior executives are asked to step aside when the organizations they lead experience miserable failures characterized by repeated poor performance. Mike Novak, the new executive director of the Texas Facilities Commission, was now in charge of a state agency with all the failing indicators: leadership and performance problems, disengagement (at all levels of the organization), low retention, roles and skills misalignment, and mismatched and fragmented operations within and between departments where employees did not collaborate and share information. The agency had multiple silos, inefficiencies, duplicated efforts, and widespread department suboptimization.

Each of these failing indicators will be addressed in this book.

Chapters 1 through 3 will discuss the elements of organizational failure mentioned above and suggest actions leaders can take to avoid these unenviable conditions. Chapters 4 through 10 introduce an advanced leadership approach to move an organization from failing and underachieving to a highly performing one that consistently meets its mission objectives. When leaders understand the power of relationships, they can move their organization's performance from poor or good to great!

Compassionate success is what great leaders strive for. It requires a Compassionate Success Mindset and the ability to build the sustaining momentum that propels an organization to a higher level of performance. Chapter 11 explains how Mike Novak achieved compassionate success and turned TFC around. He had the right mindset and built TFC's brand back by creating transformational momentum.

Reading this book will show you that the key to organizational growth depends on a leader's willingness to invest in relational capital. Let's get started.

CHAPTER 1

Leadership and Performance Problems

"No leader wakes up in the morning with the intent to be mediocre."
- Kymberli Speight

What is relational capital? It's the value an organization gains from its system of interconnected relationships - relationships that are built on trust and collective collaboration. An impactful, transformational leader must focus not just on "what" will get the job done, but also "how" it's getting done, and "who" is doing it. When leaders lose the balance of focusing between the "what," "how," and "who," projects derail, organizations miss goals, and internal relationships break down at the leadership and team member levels.

In this chapter, we'll explore the two skill areas (hard skills and soft skills) that determine how adept a leader is at balancing their time on the "what," "how," and "who." Both hard and soft skills are required to lead projects, teams, departments, and organizations.

Although this is a straightforward concept, most people focus on hard skills development. Many leaders who have climbed the ladder from supervisor to mid-level manager to department head to C-suite executives discover the critical role soft skills play in everyday executive and management decisions. The main idea is that having strong hard and soft skills is the difference between being a respected and trusted leader and an ineffective manager with the title of boss.

Hard Skills and the Gaps That Undermine Leadership

Hard skills are the technical, measurable skills and transferable experiences required to fill a leadership role. If continuing education is not a priority, over time, a leader's knowledge and experience become dated and less relevant.

A tell-tale sign of hard skill erosion is when leaders refer to their "years of experience" when challenged with a new method, process, or procedure. Another flag is when a leader becomes the "chief delegator-in-charge" and relies heavily on others to keep up with technology and industry changes.

This degradation of hard skills eventually erodes a leader's relevance, effectiveness, and credibility with their direct reports. In leadership, credibility is everything. When your team senses you're out of your depth, their confidence in your guidance, directives, and decisions wanes and eventually shifts to the mid-level manager and line supervisors. Outdated hard skills can also lead to ill-fated decisions.

Soft Skills and the Gaps That Break Trust

While a leader's hard skills help determine "what" needs to happen and "how" it should be done, soft skills help a leader take care of the people who are performing the actual work. These skills determine how well you communicate, make people feel, solve workplace problems, listen to employees, and, ultimately, how you work with and motivate people. The more developed a leader's soft skills are, the more adept they'll be at handling the daily encounters in each of these scenarios.

Soft skill gaps can be just as devastating to a leader's effectiveness as hard skill gaps and, in some cases, be a worse leadership deficit. Poor communication snowballs into misunderstandings, which lead to unmet expectations, missed deadlines, distrust in leadership and between employees, and, eventually, conflict. A leader's lack of empathy or emotional intelligence can poison a room.

I've watched leaders whose tone, delivery, or body language left their teams intimidated to the point of inaction, and feeling belittled, dismissed, or dejected.

A Tale of Two Leaders

I'll never forget two vastly different leadership moments I witnessed early in my career. In one situation, a junior executive was giving a briefing when her superior, a senior leader, didn't like what he heard. He dressed her down publicly, in front of the entire room. His tone was harsh, his words sharp, and the effect was devastating. As a young observer, I walked out of that meeting thinking, "I never want to be in her shoes. And I never want to work for him." I was tremendously intimidated by that leader.

Years later, I witnessed another senior executive respond to a disappointing situation with his team. He was firm – make no mistake, but calm, measured, and dignified as he addressed the issue. I knew he was unhappy, but he corrected us without humiliating anyone. Even though I was embarrassed as I walked out of that room, his demeanor and message instilled in me a commitment to never be in that situation again. Through this undoubtedly different approach, that leader earned respect.

The best leaders live by a simple rule: praise in public, chastise in private.

That is the power of soft skills. They give you the ability to correct without crushing - to hold people accountable without stripping them of their dignity and to lead in a way that strengthens relationships instead of shattering them. Leaders who neglect these skills do not just risk performance problems, they risk creating unhealthy work environments where mistrust and fear are the norm.

When a leader lacks good soft skills, they often create an environment where no one speaks up when "the boss" needs to hear the truth. This type of environment discourages collaborative solution development. It can be frustrating and a waste of talent. People check out. They stop offering ideas. They stop striving for excellence. Over time, you don't just lose productivity, you lose people.

Refining your soft skills will not come from classroom time but from paying attention to every human interaction you have throughout the day. If leaders make it a habit to treat everyone they encounter with respect and appreciation, chances are they'll develop exceptional soft skills.

Summary Takeaways

Great leadership isn't about always having the right answers. It's about staying humble enough to acknowledge blind spots in your skill set and staying on a continuous trajectory of improvement. Hard skills keep you competent. Soft skills keep you connected. Leaders who have high-level hard and soft skills, and have mastered maintaining a balance of both, foster work environments where trust flourishes, creative solutions are plentiful, teams thrive, and goals are met. This type of leadership is worth pursuing.

CHAPTER 2

Engagement and Retention

"At the heart of engagement and retention problems is a lack of compassionate leadership."
- Kymberli Speight

Management behavior is among the top five reasons people leave their jobs. People don't struggle with leaving a bad boss. Poor leadership can lead to disengagement and retention problems. More specifically, the problem is often a lack of compassionate leadership.

You can work for an innovative, industry-leading company, but if people feel ignored or dismissed at that company, they'll eventually walk. And the best ones will go first.

If leaders want their teams to thrive, two areas must be at the forefront of their agendas: engagement and retention.

The Power of Compassionate Leadership

Employee engagement mirrors leadership's interest in their employees. Compassionate leaders genuinely care about their employees and how employees treat each other. It's a mindset that people matter. It's the relentless pursuit of engagement and the continual fight against disengagement.

When leaders are out of touch, disengaged, or unempathetic toward the well-being of their employees, those employees stop caring. In any workforce, you'll find a spectrum of employee behavior from fully engaged to disengaged. Compassionate leadership does not guarantee employee engagement, but it provides fertile ground for it and will give a leader an acute awareness of engaged and disengaged behavior.

Compassionate leaders genuinely care about their employees and how employees treat each other.

The objective of leaders is obviously to foster employee engagement. Make no mistake, leaders are in the people business. Les Giblin describes an excellent way to facilitate engagement in his #1 international best-selling book, *How to Have Confidence and Power in Dealing with People*. He referred to this method as the "Triple-A" Technique:

- Acceptance – Accept people as they are.
- Approval – Look for something to approve of in the other person.

- Appreciation – To appreciate means to raise in value. Let people know that you value them.

When I speak about developing authentic, momentum-building relationships, I mention the three As but add one more verb: "respect" – recognizing the inherent value and importance of every person.

A leader who rarely shows they care about their employees is planting the seeds of disengagement.

Leadership disengagement is not always about big failures of disregard or disrespect. Often it's the little things – not returning emails or phone calls; not recognizing efforts that went over and above; not asking for - or even worse - prematurely shutting down the ideas of others; and not giving timely, positive, or constructive feedback. A leader who rarely shows they care about their employees is planting the seeds of disengagement.

Employee disengagement occurs when employees disengage with one another or team members disengage with other teams in the organization. This situation reveals itself when teams or departments pull in different directions, employees work more on protecting their turf than on collaboration, and people operate in silos. This produces the devastating impact of missed goals and delivery dates. It suffocates innovation and lowers morale.

Disengagement that spreads throughout departments, teams, and employees gives way to quiet quitters. These are people who put in their eight hours, as if marking time. They do the minimum and are not motivated to stay late to finish a project or help a team member who's fallen behind unless they receive additional compensation. The truth is, they'll jump ship for a better opportunity before they focus on taking every opportunity to improve their current team or department's performance.

Retention Depends on Employee Opportunities and Workplace Culture

According to the 2024 Retention Report produced by the Work Institute, the top five reasons for leaving a job were:

- Career
- Health and family
- Work/life balance
- The job itself
- Management (for the first time since 2019, this factor saw a 104% increase from 2022 to 2023)

The million-dollar question for leaders is: which of the five reasons should you focus on to strengthen retention rates? The answer: all of them. Because every employee's circumstance is unique to them, leaders must stay engaged with employees to ensure there is a solid career path for professional growth, be aware of employees' work limitations due to health and family, and understand employee expectations for work/life balance.

Realistically, you won't be able to meet the requirements of all employees, but you must figure out a way to accommodate the key team members who would be difficult to replace.

Summary Takeaways

Engagement and retention are inextricably linked objectives for leaders who are focused on building perpetually high-performing organizations and teams.

Engagement keeps people invested in an organization's successful performance. Retention ensures they stay long enough to make a positive difference.

Leaders must:

- Lead by pursuing a culture of engagement at all levels.
- Effectively smother disengagement whenever and wherever possible.
- Make retention a key leadership focus area.

High engagement and retention will not happen on their own. Leaders must deliberately work to establish and maintain these objectives. Otherwise, they'll spend more time recruiting, replacing, training, and developing people – a process that decelerates organizational accomplishments.

CHAPTER 3

People and Roles Mismatches and Avoiding the Power Grab Mentality

"As the leader goes, so does the organization."
– Kymberli Speight

It's important for an organization's vision, mission, goals, and objectives to align, but it's equally important that an individual's competency and personality align with the role and team they're assigned to. Additionally, leaders must ensure teams operate within their organizational structure alignment to avoid suboptimization and power grabs.

When There's a People Mismatch

When evaluating, hiring, and eventually assigning someone to a team, the degree to which they get along with their teammates is as important as whether they can do the job. Usually, hiring officials invest a great deal of effort into screening and ensuring a selected candidate is capable of performing the tasks and responsibilities of an unfilled position.

So I want to spend some time discussing the critical aspect of selecting and assigning people so they'll work well on the team on which they're placed.

I enjoy good music. In general, when bands break up to go their separate ways, it's usually for relational reasons. Can you recall reading an article on a band breakup because an artist lacked the talent to make good music? In sports, good players are often traded if management and the coaching staff believe they're creating a toxic environment in the locker room. Capable executives and employees leave or are asked to leave organizations because of their inability to work with one or more team members.

Engaged leaders know the individual strengths, weaknesses, and personalities of team members.

The objective is not to put together a team that has the chance for a minimum amount of conflict, but a team where competent, reasonable people can successfully produce great results and work through healthy conflict when it arises.

Engaged leaders know their teams. Not only do they know the individual strengths and weaknesses of the team members, but they also know the different personalities. Through careful assessment, leaders can assign the right fit in both hard and soft skills that enhance a team's performance. It's costly in both productivity and salaries to have smart, competent people who do not get along and don't work well with each other on the same team.

When Team Roles Are Misaligned

Leaders sometimes find themselves dealing with other departments or teams within the organization that have attempted to redefine their roles. These attempts can be a formal change in business internal policies and procedures.

It's surprising the negative impact an unnecessary additional review or validation step can have on multiple departments or teams that share interdependent processes.

Other times, it's less formal actions over time where certain leaders collude against another leader to get their way. This collusion may be driven by selfish ambition and personal gain, or a concerted effort to diminish or subordinate another leader's role and responsibilities. These collusive efforts harvest an unhealthy work environment of siloed "us vs. them" mentalities. These silos also create communication barriers that ultimately perpetuate suboptimal decisions.

Whether subordinate leaders are formally or informally attempting to redefine their roles within an organization, the result is the same. The organization is experiencing a team role misalignment crisis. You might think crisis is a strong word to use, but it's accurate because team role misalignment has a devastating effect on an organization's ability to perform efficiently and effectively. This phenomenon can cripple mission accomplishment and profit margins.

What causes this type of behavior? When you peel back the layers of dysfunctionality between departments or teams, don't be surprised to discover unhealthy relationships between two or more managers and their respective teams. There's a lack of mutual respect or trust between leaders. And, in some cases, team leaders or managers dislike one another. Poor relationships between department or team leaders can quickly morph into teams not working well together. All it takes is a disparaging or derogatory comment in a staff meeting about another team's leader or their performance, and permission has been given to "trash talk" another team, its members, or their performance.

Team role misalignment is devastating to an organization's ability to perform efficiently and effectively.

Unfortunately, this undesirable behavior between department or team leaders is a breeding ground for the power grab mentality – if I own this process or responsibility, then I control the outcome and the actions of other team leaders or managers I don't trust.

When leaders discover the behavior from team role misalignments, they're seeing symptoms of a much bigger problem. These bad relationships (amongst managers and team leaders) are destructive to organizational harmony and high team performance. Leadership disharmony destroys morale and collaboration, and, when left unchecked, an organization's success and brand.

It's like a homeowner seeing hollow, buckling, warped, or damaged wood, or discarded wing segments. Chances are that home has termites.

How do you correct team role misalignments? Find and fix the broken or dysfunctional relationships between department or team leaders and managers. Leaders must address subordinate leaders' discourteousness or disrespect for one another as soon as it happens. Immediately set the tone that, when conflict occurs, you will not tolerate an environment of winners vs. losers. Department heads and team leaders must understand that you expect a give-and-take attitude and win-win solutions.

On a daily basis, publicly point out how each of your subordinate leaders' and their respective teams' unique value, together with their fellow managers' unique value, contributes to the organization's success. Insist that all policy and procedure changes be vetted by every manager who will be affected by the proposed changes. And, when necessary, bring all relevant subordinate leaders together in a face-to-face meeting to resolve conflicts that are not being successfully worked through due to a communication breakdown or the onset of a silo mentality.

Summary Takeaways

People mismatches can disrupt a team's performance. As you see this pattern move up through the leadership ranks, you'll see siloed thinking, suboptimized decisions, and/or team role misalignments.

This behavior should be treated like a degenerative disease that must be addressed immediately. When subordinate leaders cannot find common ground and work through conflict effectively, their respective team members or departments get pulled onto the battlefield. To neutralize this negative force, leaders must set the standard and expectation that acceptance, approval, appreciation, and respect towards others is welcomed, and discourteous, disrespectful behavior towards others will be swiftly dealt with.

Assure each of your subordinate leaders of how they, and their team's unique contributions, combined with the other teams' contributions, make it possible to achieve the organization's objectives and successful performance.

Show me a situation where department and team leaders are accepting, approving, appreciating, and respecting each other, and I guarantee you their teams are working together, enhancing each team's contribution, constructively working through conflict, and developing collaborative solutions toward meeting common organizational goals and objectives.

"As the leader goes, so does the organization."

CHAPTER 4

The Compassionate Success Mindset

"The Compassionate Success Mindset means sprinting towards the goal, but not past the people."

– Kymberli Speight

In the first three chapters, we've focused on the symptoms and underlying issues for an organization's lack of performance and, in some cases, catastrophic failure. We've discussed how these circumstances can be avoided if leaders focus on the "who" as much as the "what" and "how."

With the fundamental reassertion that people make the difference, it's time to talk about how leaders can take their organization's consistently poor performance or even satisfactory performance to consistently great achievements and growth. It starts with the leader having a Compassionate Success Mindset. Okay, what does that mean? It means leaders should sprint towards their goal, but not past the people.

Notice I didn't say "their" people, but "the" people. Often, the resources a team or organization needs to successfully accomplish its objectives may not all reside within its team. There are people who will gladly share their resources if they like you, if you share, and if they know you care about their well-being.

At its core, compassionate success is not just being deadly serious about winning, but also about treating the people on your team well AND demanding they treat each other well.

The three core components of a Compassionate Success Mindset are: *finding a why that's bigger than you, embracing being uncomfortable, and taking every opportunity to give without expectation.* A leader needs a compelling and urgent reason to lead a team to sprint towards a worthwhile achievement. One that will require team members to ignore the uncomfortable tasks and mentally challenging and physically exhausting experiences along the journey, while not ignoring their team's individual needs or pushing people that are in their path out of the way.

Component One: When Your Why Is Bigger Than You

Many people talk about the importance of your why. But I take it a little further. I ask: "Is your why big enough?" The reason I take this next step is because of personal experience. Here's what I mean. Sometimes obstacles get in your way, life happens, or your motivation wanes. You're making progress, but all of a sudden, things come to a halt. When that happens, go back to your why. Is your why big enough to help you get through the tough times? And that usually means your why has to be bigger than you. If it's just something you want, you might start going after it, but when things get hard, maybe you don't give that extra push. But if your why is bigger than you, you'll have even more resolve to see it through. You'll do what it takes to figure it out.

When I first set out to help senior military leaders in career transition, I didn't know how I was going to accomplish that. I didn't have the expertise or credentials to do it, and I didn't have access, at scale, to those I wanted to help. But I had a "why bigger than me." I started my own company, made connections, and got the training and experience I needed. My company now runs the Executive Transition Assistance Program (ETAP) across the Air Force.

As a leader, helping your team develop a big why can fuel them. Take time to get to know and understand "who" your team members are and "what" motivates them. You may need to regularly point out how your organization successfully delivers your product or service and is now helping many recipients.

When your "why" is bigger than you, you'll do the uncomfortable work and push through setbacks.

Having a Compassionate Success Mindset means having the conviction to accomplish corporate objectives that will positively impact many. When your why is bigger than you — when it's about the people you serve, the team you're developing, or the community you're impacting — the facts don't matter. You'll figure it out. You'll do the uncomfortable work, and you'll push through setbacks because your motivation isn't just about personal gain; it's about something greater.

In the next chapter, we'll discuss what it means to find and sustain a why that's bigger than you. The greater your reasons for accomplishing an objective, the stronger you'll stand when challenges inevitably come.

Component Two: Embracing Being Uncomfortable

Growth rarely happens in your comfort zone. Every leader will face times when the going gets tough. When these situations arise, squared-away leaders power through these stormy seasons of leadership while others practice their version of "stress transference."

When you're experiencing the latter leadership coping behavior, you'll hear comments like, "The boss isn't happy." Or, "Is it safe to go in?" Dealing effectively with uncomfortable moments – taking uncomfortable risks, having uncomfortable conversations, and making necessary but uncomfortable changes—is an indispensable trait in a leader with a Compassionate Success Mindset.

Growth rarely happens in your comfort zone.

Shirzad Chamine, author of *Positive Intelligence*, talks about the importance of getting familiar with your internal triggers — the negative voices that creep in when you're stressed or uncertain. You know the ones: "What if I fail? What if I'm not good enough? What if this blows up in my face?" If you don't know how to recognize and quiet those voices, you'll shrink back from the very situations that could make you stronger. In Chapter 6, we'll unpack this concept in detail.

Component Three: Take Every Opportunity to Give Without Expectation

The third element of the Compassionate Success Mindset might be the simplest — while also being the hardest. It's about giving freely, without keeping score. The most effective leaders are givers. They share knowledge. They invest in people. They open doors. And they do it without the silent contract that says, "Now you owe me one."

Having ulterior motives erodes trust. If I only support you because I secretly expect something from you in return, you'll feel that — even if I never say it out loud. When people know you're investing in them simply because you want a good outcome for them, loyalty and trust grow.

The most effective leaders are givers.

It's similar to planting seeds. You don't plant a seed one day and demand fruit the next morning. You plant it, you water it, and you trust that in time, it will bear something good. Giving without expectation works the same way. You may not see immediate returns, and the benefit may not even come back to you directly from where you originally planted the seeds. But in the long run, generosity creates ecosystems of trust and support that are far more sustainable than the transactional "I'll scratch your back if you scratch mine" approach.

In Chapter 7, we'll discuss what this looks like in practice and look at a real-world example of a leader who gave freely and the fruitful outcome that generosity created. Being a giver is a strength and one of the clearest markers of a compassionate leader.

Summary Takeaways

The three elements of the Compassionate Success Mindset are:

1. Having a "why" bigger than you
2. Embracing being uncomfortable
3. Taking every opportunity to give without expectation

These elements aren't quick tips or leadership hacks. They're ways of thinking and being that transform how you show up — for yourself and your organization.

Compassionate success and, by extension, compassionate leadership, means having a mindset that success matters, people matter, growth matters, and trust matters.

CHAPTER 5

When Your Why Is Bigger Than You

*"When your why is bigger than you, you lead with
the confidence that the achievement
is worth the collective effort."*

– Kymberli Speight

There will always be moments when life asks more of us than we believe we can possibly give. We're constantly faced with new challenges or unexpected obstacles at work or in our personal lives. For leaders, it could be the weight of having a vision that your staff hasn't accepted or supported. When this occurs, how do leaders keep their vision burning hot enough to ignite the flame in others? In other words, is the why big enough to persevere?

Your why is the reason for showing up and pushing through when quitting looks easier or as the more rational path to take. Finding your purpose is good. However, for organizations and teams to accomplish great feats, I believe that purpose must be a shared, bigger-than-you purpose. Often, having a purpose is focused on a goal or objective you want to achieve, while having a purpose or a why bigger than you indicates there are many who will benefit from your success.

Pushing Through to the Other Side

At some point in your life, if you haven't already, you'll face a wall that feels insurmountable. In that moment, your why will either propel you over the wall or, if it's not big enough, leave you transfixed with fear and regret. If you can't figure out a way over, under, around, or through that obstacle, regardless of how long or how many attempts it takes to negotiate this impediment, chances are your why isn't big enough. I'm not judging you, just giving you a point of reflection.

My Why Guided Me Through

Years ago, my mentor, who had poured her knowledge and wisdom into me, began encouraging me to fly solo - deliver a four-day seminar to senior-level executives without her. This thought intimidated me, and I kept putting it off. I was more comfortable co-teaching with her. Then one day she called and said, "Kym, I apologize, this has never happened before, but I double-booked two courses. I hate to ask, but can you be at the second location tomorrow and lead the seminar?"

Without hesitation, I said yes! I immediately got off the phone, booked my flight, hotel, and rental car, and packed. I was on a plane within hours. I arrived at my hotel room after midnight and was ready to start the seminar at 7:30 the next morning. I don't mind telling you I was more than a little uncomfortable. But I had to embrace this first-time experience leading a seminar in front of a room full of seasoned senior military leaders - some of the most direct and unvarnished communicators who would not have hesitated to let me know if I was wasting their time.

What allowed me to lean into this intimidating experience? My why being bigger than me kicked in! My mentor was calling, and she needed help. I wasn't about to let her down. Secondly, I would be teaching and coaching senior military executives on how to successfully transition from military to civilian employment – another "why bigger than me" that had developed after watching my husband, with two master's degrees and a transferable skillset, face difficulty in finding his right fit. While we went through his transition, my recurring thought was that it shouldn't be this hard for capable military executives who have faithfully served their country for 20 years or more to show civilian employers their invaluable knowledge, skills, and work ethic.

When I found myself on a plane to do my first course without my mentor, I was confident I'd made the right decision. I knew I was exactly where I needed to be because I was on a mission to help others.

Another reason for having a why bigger than you is the fact that once we accomplish our goals, there's the possibility of becoming complacent. Through the years, I've observed a level of disillusionment in my life and in others when we finally accomplish, achieve, acquire, or gain the experience we wanted. The funny thing is, I've never felt disillusioned when I've gone on a mission trip or been a part of something serving others.

This is the power of searching for a why bigger than yourself. It allows you to see past the obstacle to your desired outcome, regardless of its size or complexity.

I'm not a golfer. But my husband tells me golfers don't focus on the hazards or sand traps, but on the green where the flag is. Because when you focus on those obstacles where you don't want your ball to go, that's often where it does go.

When a leader has a "why bigger than me" mentality and the organization embraces it, there's no limit to what can and will be accomplished because of the collective belief that achieving the mission and objectives will positively affect others.

Summary Takeaways

Leaders, having a "why bigger than me" is not about lofty inspiration; it's about daily choices to look past or through obstacles and impediments to the objectives the team is working to achieve.

If you find yourself or your employees stuck and consistently looking at obstacles, regulations, business conditions, and other barriers in the way of accomplishing the mission, then perhaps the why is simply not big enough. The truth is, a big why is about the lives you'll positively impact when your organization perseveres through the obstacles to the collective desired end-state.

CHAPTER 6

Embrace Being Uncomfortable: It's Part of the Deal

"If you want compassionate success, become comfortable with being uncomfortable."
– Kymberli Speight

Accepting the Unavoidable

Growth and achievement are not friends with stagnation, regression, or failure. But they are inextricably related to each other like heads and tails on a coin. Reading these first two sentences, you might ask where average and mediocrity fit in? In my opinion, they don't belong beside growth and achievement. Shareholders, Boards of Directors, and entrepreneurs would not link growth and achievement with mediocrity either. Leaders must accept the unavoidable truth that they have been selected to fill their role to lead growth and achievement.

When was the last time you heard a senior executive introduced with words like "...we're excited to bring him on board to keep us focused on maintaining the status quo" or "we're glad she joined the team and are looking forward to her mediocre leadership?" You never will because everyone knows stagnation leads to regression that ends in failure. If we understand these truths, why are there more average-performing and failing organizations than high-performing organizations with an expanding brand presence?

Peeling back the layers of reasons for an organization's mediocre or failing performance, you'll discover that at the core is the avoidance of uncomfortable leadership decisions – the avoidance of taking risks, making tough staffing changes, and having uncomfortable conversations about employee performance. Leaders sometimes spend more time and energy trying to avoid controversy and keep their jobs out of jeopardy than making tough calls.

For the remainder of this chapter, I want to spend some time discussing the sabotaging thoughts behind the decisions we make.

Get to the Root of Your Thoughts

Some of the invisible roadblocks in our thought patterns find their way into every decision we make and every conversation we have. When I ask executives what's holding them back, they often pause and realize they haven't taken the time to think about it. So, take the time right now to stop for one minute and analyze what you think about. Literally time yourself.

Welcome back. I hope you completed this exercise.

Your self-talk shapes how you show up. If your root thought is, "I'm not enough" or "I'm in over my head," you'll see those beliefs coloring every conversation you have and every team you lead. Unwittingly, you'll play small, second-guess yourself, or attempt to overcompensate. If your root thought is "My staff can't be trusted," you'll micromanage them and unintentionally stifle productivity.

For good decision-making, do your best to bring those subconscious thoughts forward by asking yourself:

- What assumptions am I making about this situation?
- What story am I telling myself right now?
- Is this story true?

In everyday conversation, there are preconceived thoughts or notions – formed opinions that lack proof or evidence. For the next tough decision you're faced with, ask yourself why you feel uncomfortable.

- Is it because you don't want to make the wrong decision and look less intelligent and competent?
- Is it because the right decision might stir up controversy?
- Are you afraid to say "I don't know" or "I'm not prepared to make this decision right now?"
- Are you less than enthused to deal with the people involved?

If you're honest, you'll discover a level of awareness that will lead you to the right decision for the right reasons. It will also help you feel confident to make unpopular decisions with empathy.

Diminish Your Inner Saboteurs

Another area that will affect your decisions and judgment is from Shirzad Chamine's book *Positive Intelligence*. In it, Chamine describes how we protect the thoughts we learned as children that served us well, but now, as adults, act as saboteurs.

If you've ever wrestled with perfectionism, people-pleasing, or self-doubt, you've met some saboteurs firsthand. Most of us are unaware of how our mind sabotages us daily with our unconscious thoughts caused by saboteurs.

These saboteurs started as survival mechanisms in childhood and helped us cope, protect ourselves, or receive love. They're anchored to significant childhood emotional events and tend to be the stronger thoughts that come out when we're in crisis, fight or flight mode as adults. I know people who have kept certain thoughts long past their usefulness because they grew up during the depression. I also consider these thoughts to be major threats to work and personal relationships.

Here is a list of the saboteurs we, as adults, must consciously manage:

- Judge – harshly criticizing yourself, others, and circumstances
- Controller – needing to dominate every outcome
- Hyper–achiever – tying your worth to constant success

- Stickler – obsessing over perfection and order
- Pleaser – over-serving others to earn approval
- Hyper-vigilant – always on edge, expecting the worst
- Avoider – dodging conflict and discomfort
- Victim – feeling powerless and resigned
- Hyper-rational – dismissing feelings in favor of cold logic
- Restless – constantly chasing the next thing

The good news is we don't have to let these voices run the show forever. Diminishing the impact of saboteurs begins with awareness. Chamine offers a free Positive Intelligence assessment that identifies your strongest saboteurs. Scan the QR code below to access the assessment:

Scan me

I recommend you take this assessment to understand which saboteur thoughts are most negatively influencing your conversations and decisions. Once you know your strongest saboteurs, you can start working to lessen their grip. The goal isn't to eliminate them entirely – they'll always whisper from time to time – but to quiet their power so you can make decisions more intentionally.

The wiser self is what Chamine calls the Sage Mind. Instead of reacting from the amygdala part of your brain, which operates from fear, scarcity, or judgment, you want to operate from the Sage Mind, which lives in the middle prefrontal cortex. The Sage Mind acts with empathy, creativity, and courage. It sees challenges and obstacles as opportunities to grow, instead of threats it must survive.

Chamine's five key Sage powers:

1. Empathize – showing compassion, appreciation, and forgiveness to yourself and others
2. Explore – staying curious
3. Innovate – generating many ideas that can lead to fresh and innovative solutions
4. Navigate – aligning decisions with your deeper values
5. Activate – taking bold action once the path is clear

When you diminish your saboteurs and strengthen your Sage Mind, you create space for better decisions, deeper relationships, and more resilient leadership.

Everyone, including leaders, has these inner battles. The difference between feeling diminished or overwhelmed and making safe, comfortable decisions, feeling empowered, and taking smart risks to make bold decisions that lead to your organization's growth and achievement, is whether we let the saboteurs drive us or whether we hand the keys to the Sage Mind.

Summary Takeaways

Self-awareness is good. However, if you want to truly embrace the idea of becoming comfortable with being uncomfortable, you must master the saboteur thoughts that negatively influence your decisions. Leaders need clear minds to explore, navigate, innovate, activate, and empathize. Challenge yourself to take Chamine's free assessment and learn which saboteurs you need to diminish and see the opportunities for growth versus the daily obstacles and impediments threatening your organization's success. The leaders who thrive when situations are uncomfortable, when unpleasant decisions or tasks must be performed, aren't fearless; they've just learned how to effectively manage their internal saboteurs.

CHAPTER 7

Take Every Opportunity to Give Without Expectation

"The real power of relationships comes when you give freely, without the expectation of receiving anything in return, but because you want to give and because you can."
– Kymberli Speight

I've learned something about great relationships that no textbook or corporate workshop could have ever taught me: the most transformative moments happen when you give without keeping score. You give without thinking about favors you can cash in later – you're not thinking about strategy or leverage.

True giving – the kind that creates trust, loyalty, and growth – happens when you offer your time and talents without expecting anything in return. But you do get something back – it's the relationship itself.

This can feel counterintuitive in today's world, where so many of our interactions are transactional. We're used to exchanging time for money, ideas for credit, and help for recognition. But the real power of leadership comes when you give because you want to, because you can, because it's the right thing to do, and because people matter.

Why Mike Novak Became Executive Director of the Texas Facility Commission — Giving Without Expectation

Mike Novak did not need a job, and he didn't need to work when he accepted the executive director position at the Texas Facilities Commission. He had over 35 years of entrepreneurial experience in starting and developing award-winning construction firms. He served a four-year term as a Bexar County Commissioner, and Ernst & Young named him the 1992 Entrepreneur of the Year.

However, Novak's strong belief in giving without expectation compelled him to serve on many boards and associations in San Antonio, Texas. He was Chairman of the Board of the Greater San Antonio Chamber of Commerce, Chairman of the Board of Morningside Ministries, and Tri-Chair, with senior military generals, of the San Antonio Military Task Force for nine years. All totaled, he served on more than 10 boards or commissions as chairman, vice chair, or president.

Clearly, Novak had enough financial success, awards, and recognition, and served in multiple distinguished positions. No one would have faulted him if he had said, "I'm not your guy. It's time for me to enjoy my grandkids."

But he didn't. Why? Because he felt an obligation to give back. He saw the executive director's role as a great opportunity to be a public servant once again. This was another way he could share his wealth of construction and business knowledge and experience.

Because Novak has given generously of his time outside of running his business, he has developed a massive network of capable, successful individuals who will answer his phone call and give back to him when he needs their help. His personal and professional networks allow him to generate an impressive amount of momentum. We'll discuss in Chapter 10 how important it is for leaders to generate momentum.

As a leader, you have a choice every day: will you operate from a place of scarcity or generosity? Will you guard your resources or trust that generosity multiplies them?

The leaders who lean into generosity end up not only with stronger teams, resources, and connections, but also with a deeper sense of personal fulfillment.

Summary Takeaways

Taking every opportunity to give without expectation is not a leadership tactic – it's a way of living. You're not attempting to pander future favor from others. Giving ignites generosity that promotes authentic, long-lasting relationships - and that's a key element to building momentum.

CHAPTER 8

Building Authentic Relationships

"When people know, like, and trust you, they don't just work with you – they open doors for you."
– Kymberli Speight

When I first began my professional career after college, I noticed there were a lot of people who were what I call smoozers – people trying to get ahead and be the movers and shakers in their peer groups. They wanted to be in the "right" meetings with the "right" decision makers. In short, these people were jockeying for personal gain.

Decades later, I still see a significant amount of his type of behavior, and some people have gotten ahead with this approach. I would classify relationships formed this way as transactional and often inauthentic.

There is a Better Way

When you build authentic relationships in which individuals value the other person and not what they can do for each other, the relationship has a chance to be transformational.

Transformational relationships produce synergy – the collective result of people working together that far exceeds the individual effects of them working alone. The common element in all transformational relationships is trustworthiness. This is the sentiment people have that you're trustworthy – that you're not only looking out for your own best interest, but also the best interest of the other person and of the relationship – the shared "bigger than me" why.

Let's analyze the components of trustworthiness and their relationship with each other.

The Trust Equation

Charles H. Green, credited with developing the trust equation, framed it this way:

$$\text{Trustworthiness} = \frac{\text{Credibility} + \text{Reliability} + \text{Intimacy}}{\text{Self-Orientation}}$$

Let's break down what these terms mean:

- Credibility – a person is competent, capable, and has relevant credentials (a subject matter expert). Does the person project confidence? Do we feel and believe that the person is telling us the truth?

- Reliability – trust that the person will do what they said they would. Do they have a good track record? Are they consistent? Does the person understand our frame of reference, so when they promise us something, they understand what we mean?
- Intimacy – feeling emotional security in dealing with us. Do we feel safe sharing information with that person? Is there confidence that the person will handle that information respectfully and appropriately (emotional intelligence, vulnerability, empathy)?
- Self-Orientation – the amount of time you focus on yourself and what you want (selfishness, self-obsession).

Green and his team broke trustworthiness into the four components to provide a more practical way to think about how to increase or enhance your level of trustworthiness.

The Trust Equation

"This equation is just a model to get us thinking about trust and trustworthiness."

"You get more benefit from addressing your weaknesses than from increasing your strengths. Because we perceive that someone who is consistent across all four components is balanced, whole, complete, and in sync. By contrast, someone who is imbalanced across the four components is perceived as lacking in coherence, consistency, and balance – at odds with what we want in someone to trust."

– Charles H. Green, Trusted Advisor Associates

Others Focused vs. Me Focused 3-Score Challenge

Here is a method for applying Green's trustworthiness equation:

$$\text{Trustworthiness} = \frac{\text{Credibility} + \text{Reliability} + \text{Intimacy}}{\text{Self-Orientation}}$$

How this works:

1. Assign each component to the right side of the equation a value based on whatever scale makes sense to you. (Examples: 1 is low and 10 is high, or 10 is low and 100 is high.)

2. If we assume a person has balance and is in sync across all four components, they would score a perfect 3.

$$\text{Others focused } 3 = \frac{10 + 10 + 10}{10}$$

3. However, let's assume someone is imbalanced and lacking consistency across all four components, and they scored higher in the self-oriented component than in the other three components. This time, when you run the calculation, the result will be less than 3.

Example:

$$\text{Me focused } 2.6 = \frac{9 + 9 + 8}{10}$$

(The greater the negative difference between a 3 score and your score gives you an indicator to what degree you are me focused.)

4. Remember: It's important to realize the objective isn't to achieve scores greater than 3. Scores that are higher than or lower than indicate an imbalance in how you're being perceived. Scores higher than 3 may mean you're not maintaining a healthy self-orientation. You might be perceived as a people pleaser or someone who can't say no when it's appropriate to do so.

Why It Makes Sense to Build Authentic Relationships

Authentic relationships are transformational in many ways. We weren't created to live life alone. What if the next person you meet today is the exact person you need to know tomorrow? Or perhaps they need to know you. Down the road, you won't know how you can be of help to others or how they can be of help to you.

Make no mistake, the beauty is in the relationship itself, but you never know where your help may come from. This is far from transactional.

Summary Takeaways

There is a better way to live life and obtain success than by being a smoozer! Make it a point to develop authentic relationships built on trust. Consider investing time to read the book, The Trusted Advisor by David H. Maister, Charles H. Green, and Robert M. Galford, to assess and enhance your trustworthiness.

Are you more me focused? Or do you have a healthy balance between your wants and others? For an additional resource, I recommend the book Can I Trust You? by Scott Carley.

NOTE: When building trust, it's appropriate to address your weaknesses. When building your personal brand, the appropriate strategy is to focus on your strengths and only address weaknesses to the extent they get in the way of achieving your goals.

CHAPTER 9

Building Momentum that Leads to Big Results

"If you want organizational growth,
you must invest in relational capital."
– Kymberli Speight

In the past, Microsoft, Apple, and Coca-Cola have all made changes or additions to their executive staff to increase growth. In a 2017 WIRED article, Greg Williams describes how Microsoft got its "groove back" by hiring a new CEO. In 2013, Apple announced the creation of a new position, a senior vice president who would be reporting directly to the CEO and provide oversight and strategic direction, expansion, and operation of retail and online stores. In 2016, Coca-Cola hired a new CEO to focus on delivering higher margins.

What do these three examples have in common? They are Organizations that we're seeking to attain momentum towards growth and higher margins. In general, every organization aims to achieve its mission, goals, and objectives with continuously increased efficiency and effectiveness. In cases where an organization is not performing well or its performance is declining, executive leadership takes action to generate positive momentum.

The point is, in addition to having a Compassionate Success Mindset, you, as a leader, must also understand how to generate momentum in your organization. When leaders show up every day with clarity on why it's important for the organization to succeed, are willing and prepared to do the uncomfortable tasks, and are modeling to employees the practice of taking every opportunity to give without expectation, they're fostering a winning culture. However, to attain and sustain the momentum necessary for accelerated growth or improvement, it frequently requires someone new – someone with new perspectives, talents, and a skillset the organization doesn't have.

The Social Science Momentum Equation

Amongst the many engineering and science courses I took at the Air Force Academy, there was a physics equation that stuck with me over the years, specifically the linear momentum equation ($p=mv$) derived from Sir Isaac Newton's laws. As I thought about the relationship between how many people you know and the value of those relationships, I had an epiphany – these are the two components necessary to build the momentum required to accomplish big projects and goals that require collective efforts. The more interesting thought I had was that the relationship of **mass times velocity equals linear momentum** paralleled the concept of how the **number of people you know times the value of those relationships**

equals the momentum that drives productivity. Let me explain further.

Intuitively, leaders have used this concept of adding or changing staff to increase results for years. But now I want to introduce a way to use this strategy more universally through viewing the linear momentum equation, $p=mv$. In the physics application:

- p – *Momentum*
- m – *Mass*
- v – *Velocity (vector with both magnitude and direction)*

From this basic equation, it made sense to me that the elements in the physics momentum equation have the same relationship as the elements that produce momentum in the business world. In other words, there's a parallel Social Science Momentum Equation.

What is the Social Science Momentum Equation, and how does it work?

The formula for social science momentum is:

$$Ps = m \, |Vr|$$

- *Ps – Momentum for success (The measurable rate at which a goal or objective is accomplished.)*
- *m – Mass (The number of relationships an individual has.)*
- *$|Vr|$ – Velocity (The "absolute" or mutual value those relationships generate.* How much non-negative beneficial value you <u>and</u> others get from these relationships.)

Building Momentum

Social Science Momentum Equation

$$P_s = m |v_r|$$

Essentially, this equation formalizes the age-old saying, "Who you know matters" or "It's not what you know but who you know."

Microsoft and Coca-Cola formally established a new relationship with different CEOs. They focused on the $|v_r|$ variable to build momentum. Apple, on the other hand, increased its staff, creating the new senior vice president role. They increased "m" by adding a relationship to their executive leadership team while simultaneously focusing on $|v_r|$.

The Social Science Momentum Equation is based on two of the three Sir Isaac Newton theories that influenced the development of the momentum physics equation.

Business World Applications of Newton's Laws

Converting Newton's well-known laws and the momentum equation to business world conditions provides a clear correlation between these distinctly different scientific applications.

Law of Inertia (1st Law)

An object at rest will stay at rest, and an object in motion will stay in motion with the same speed and in the same direction unless acted upon by an unbalanced force.

The end-state of any desired accomplishment or outcome: Without any outside decisions and influences, teams and businesses can become stagnant and nonproductive.

and

Law of Interaction (3rd Law)

For every action, there is an equal and opposite reaction. When one object exerts a force on another, the second object exerts a force of equal magnitude and opposite direction on the first.

The net effect of human interactions: Positive and negative interactions with others and the actions of team members or coworkers can have a net positive or negative effect on the team's performance, accomplishments, and work environment. Maintaining a positive environment is critical for high-level teamwork, performance, and long-term success.

The concept of a Social Science Momentum Equation is exciting news not only for leaders, but also for anyone looking to build momentum in their professional or personal life.

The more people you know - "m" times the absolute or mutual value - "$|Vr|$" that each of your relationships generates, will determine the rate at which goals or objectives are accomplished. For leaders, this means if your teams are underperforming or stagnant and you have a well-trained and motivated staff, you need to look outside your organization for that single or additional value-added relationship(s) to propel your teams forward. If your job search has gone stale, meet some new people and build a bigger network. Try it - it works!

*A Note of Caution:

Understanding "|Vr|" is critical! Without the absolute value sign, the equation lends itself to transactional behavior. "If you do this, I'll do that." Or, "If I meet the 'right person' with the 'right connections,' I can solve my problem or accomplish my goal." No, the goal is to give more than you take. The more you are a giver, the more good that comes your way. Sometimes, that good is the way you feel when you help someone in need. There are several evidence-based studies listed in the reference section that show this to be true.

The Social Science Momentum Equation was reinforced by the raw power I discovered in meeting and building relationships when I met 100 people in 100 days. I gained access to fresh and unique perspectives on life and came across many people who had talent, skillsets, and technical expertise I didn't have. The people I met shared their wisdom and graciously shared contacts from their professional and personal networks with me.

A common trait I've found in every effective and successful leader I've met or worked with is the ability to create momentum through their extensive professional and personal networks. Mike Novak, the executive from the Texas Facilities Commission I introduced you to earlier, is no exception.

Achieving compassionate success is sprinting towards your goal, but not past the people. As we addressed in Chapter 7, the third element of a leader having the Compassionate Success Mindset is *taking every opportunity to give without expectation.* If a relationship does not provide *mutual* value to all the parties involved, the absolute value decreases. A smaller "$|Vr|$" will eventually decrease momentum because relationships won't last, thus declining your rate of success.

Real-World Application of the Social Science Momentum Equation

Think about the relationship between the elements of the equation: $Ps = m \ |Vr|$.

The **rate** at which a goal or objective is accomplished is equal to the **number of relationships** an individual has **multiplied** by the **absolute** or **mutual value** those relationships generate.

Scenario #1

If you have a small network of relationships, your "m" will be small. Therefore, the momentum you generate will be limited and heavily dependent on "$|Vr|$"- the mutual value of those relationships. If the mutual value of relationships is low, chances are you'll generate limited to no momentum.

Scenario #2

If you have a large network – "*m*" and many of the relationships are superficial (i.e., provide little mutual value), you'll be able to leverage a limited level of momentum.

Scenario #3

If you have a large network with high-quality relationships (i.e., relationships with high-impact difference makers who share ideas, resources, and often give access to their robust networks), you'll generate a significant level of momentum. Thus, your rate of accomplishment and goal achievement will be accelerated.

Summary Takeaways

Leaders can build momentum that accelerates their organization or teams' success by utilizing Newton's laws and the physics equation - $p=mv$ - in a transformational way! By converting the Laws of Inertia and Interaction from physics conditions to social science conditions, a new equation emerges - $P_s = m |V_r|$ - in which momentum is determined by the number of relationships you have and the mutual value of those relationships.

As the saying goes, it's not what you know but who you know.

CHAPTER 10

Connections Matter!

"What if the next person that comes across your path today is the exact person you need to know tomorrow?"
– Kymberli Speight

Published studies and articles from the New York Times, the Harvard Business Review, Gallup, Taylor-Chadwick, and others provide many statistics that support the theme of this chapter, that connections matter. (Please see the reference section.) Here are just a few of those statistics:

- 65% of business growth depends on relationships.
- 84% of business-to-business (B2B) buyer purchases are initiated by a referral.
- Peer recommendations influence over 90% of all B2B buying decisions.
- 70% of team engagement is directly linked to a manager's actions and behaviors.
- Employees connected to a strong corporate culture are 55% less likely to actively seek other job opportunities.

Begin Developing a Network of Business Relationships

I frequently coach and consult military executives on how to build high levels of momentum that lead to an accelerated hiring process for civilian executive roles. I remind them that it was not only competence and sustained high job performance that helped them achieve their senior non-commissioned and commissioned officer rank, but also their strong networks. I explain how their networks, intertwined with decision makers' networks, resulted in deliberate actions that ensured their promotion to ranks that only 2-4% of all officers and only 1% of enlisted members achieve.

Then I give these executive job seekers their biggest assignment for developing a strong civilian job search campaign. I ask them to begin developing their network of relationships that will eventually intertwine with corporate or business decision makers' networks. In short, I tell them that if they can quickly and effectively accomplish this assignment, they will have generated the most effective momentum they need to get past the massive human resources screening process - a process that is specifically designed to pare down the hundreds of applicants who apply.

Often, dedicated senior military executives have spent the majority of their professional careers in their specialized areas of expertise, successfully leading the men and women under their command. The typical responses I hear from leaders are that their civilian circle of professional friends is limited due to deployments and the demands of being a military service member. So to prove to my seminar attendees how easy it is to meet new people, I challenged myself to meet 100 people in 100 days. What an eye-opening and rewarding experience that was! I was able to demonstrate the fundamental concept of building momentum through learning how to meet people and build meaningful, authentic relationships.

Senior-level seasoned executives (both military and corporate) know how to develop strong relationships. It's a skill that has become second nature to most. However, many junior leaders have not yet mastered this critical skill. The remainder of this chapter is aimed at providing senior executives with some fundamental and familiar relationship-building principles to facilitate their mentoring efforts.

The Components of Building a Great Relationship

In Chapter 9, I introduced the Social Science Momentum Equation — $Ps = m|Vr|$. I said the $|Vr|$ is critical because the absolute value brackets around the Vr represent a non-negative beneficial value for either party in the relationship. In other words, a mutually beneficial relationship for both parties. I also pointed out that a smaller $|Vr|$ will eventually decrease momentum because relationships won't last, thus declining your rate of success. So let's focus on how to generate a large $|Vr|$ — great relationships.

Prior to completing my 100-day challenge, I would, like you probably do, describe a great relationship from personal experience. If I were asked how this great relationship happened, I'd say "we just clicked," or "we have a lot in common," or "circumstances brought us together over time." All are valid responses. However, if you're trying to rapidly build momentum and rapport with others towards collective engagement and goal accomplishment, developing the "we clicked" factor or relatability effect takes skill and the true desire to be interested in others.

In my book, *I Need to Know You*, I break down the components of rapidly building authentic relationships. They are **Building Social Capital + Being Mindful + Paying Attention to Each Stakeholder Interaction.** I won't attempt to explain my two-hour workshop here, but my book or workshop is not for smoozers, or users, as I call them.

The basic principle is that building relationships or networking is most effective when people focus on what they can give versus what they can get. Stated in the context of the Social Science Momentum Equation:

$|Vr|$ = Building Social Capital + Being Mindful + Paying Attention to Each Stakeholder Interaction

Social Capital

Social Capital is the value you offer someone, other than monetary means. It's not what you value necessarily, but what is valuable to the other person. For different people, it could be different things. It could be your willingness to share your knowledge, expertise, insight, connections, a compliment, encouragement, time, or a host of other resources. You build social capital by being willing to give more than you take. Referring to Chapter 9 and our word of caution, this model is not transactional giving.

Being Mindful

Being Mindful means intentionally being aware and acknowledging the people that come across your path. In your day-to-day walk through life, you cross paths with many people on the way to work, such as the person you run into after parking your car, the person on an elevator, or someone from another department. Whether your work is done at the office or remotely, you may also encounter people on a virtual call. Every instance represents opportunities to engage or ignore. These are opportunities to increase the number of possible connections that could lead to great relationships. Don't forget that each of these people know other people you don't know now but might want to know at some point.

Paying Attention to Each Stakeholder Interaction

Paying Attention to Each Stakeholder Interaction is being ultra-observant during engagements, meetings, casual conversations, and social media interactions. Notice how you make the other person feel. Are you receiving confirmations that you're being genuine? Are you seeing tangible signs that tell you they believe you really care about them? This applies to both face-to-face and digital and virtual interactions. Before I hit the enter or send key on an email or text, along with checking for accurate content, good grammar, and syntax,

I look to see if the tone of my message is respectful and situationally appropriate.

Backing Up Your Words With Your Actions

Another question: Are my actions backing up my words? When a colleague loses a parent or something unfortunate happens, taking the time to check on them, sending a card or flowers (or a plant), or attending the funeral goes a long way. Some people have emailed me a picture of the Peace Lily plant I sent the very day they received it. Others have professed profound gratitude that I would come to the funeral.

People are thrilled when you show up for the good times, but when you're there for them in their time of need, that speaks volumes. It's the personal touch that shows them you care. Showing others that what's important to them is also important to you is walking the walk.

An area in which I see junior leaders miss the boat, and is therefore a great area for mentoring, is how they handle suggestions when they're holding a meeting. If someone makes a suggestion, regardless of whether the junior leader thinks it's an idea they'll implement, do they make that person feel their input was taken seriously? If their team member feels their idea was valued, even if it's not ultimately implemented, that member will continue to contribute, but if not, members will shut down and keep their other ideas to themselves. And this can happen quickly. It's the details that matter.

Applying these simple relationship concepts of Building Social Capital, Being Mindful, and Paying Attention to Each Stakeholder Interaction can help you quickly build new, authentic relationships based on trust. At my final count, six years after my challenge, I was still in contact to varying degrees with over 70 of the people I met during my 100-day challenge. Many of those new connections have been mutually beneficial across a wide spectrum of professional and personal interests.

Before I close this chapter, there's one tip I have for conventions, conferences, symposiums, and major corporate gatherings. All these events represent fruitful opportunities to increase your m|Vr|. When attending these types of events, make it your aim to walk away with quality over quantity. Instead of leaving the event with a lot of contacts, focus on establishing good rapport with fewer people so that if you were to email, text, or call, or if one of them contacted you, both of you would remember the initial meeting and discussion. I found this method to be much more rewarding and successful than the mass meet approach.

Summary Takeaways

Published studies and articles from the New York Times, the Harvard Business Review, Gallup, Taylor-Chadwick, and others provide many statistics supporting the concept that relationships help drive business growth. Therefore, the key to accelerated growth is through leaders who understand how to more quickly develop great relationships - |Vr|.

Great relationships have a non-negative beneficial value for either party or are mutually beneficial. To build authentic, trusting relationships quickly, it takes skill in applying three basic principles — Building Social Capital + Being Mindful + Paying Attention to Each Stakeholder Interaction.

CHAPTER 11

Mike Novak's Successful Journey – A Case Study of Compassionate Success and Building Momentum

"We are in the people business."
– Mike Novak

Mike Novak's Transformational Leadership

Prior to Mike Novak's arrival at the Texas Facilities Commission, leadership had been about power plays, titles, and control. People clung to their silos and fought for scraps of influence. Basic HR practices – like recognizing employees who had served the state for decades – were neglected. The focus wasn't on people; it was on egos.

But Novak took a different approach - he invested heavily in TFC's relational capital.

In the first five minutes of a conversation with Mike Novak, you gain a clear understanding of what he's all about - people. He starts many of his discussions by asking, "Do you know?" "She's the mayor of" or "He and I served on a board together." Then he explains how that particular relationship influenced or will influence a situation that's being discussed. Before your conversation is over, chances are you'll hear this statement - "We are in the people business."

One year after the commissioners removed TFC's prior executive director, they found the perfect candidate – a Navy captain with world-class facilities management experience. But right before he accepted the position, he received another offer that was too good to pass on, especially considering the location of that job offer was near his first new grandchild.

It was time for the commission to execute Plan B. Little did Vice Chairman Mike Novak know the internal search meant he was the target candidate. Novak, a lifelong entrepreneur from San Antonio, had built and sold successful construction companies and carried deep relationships across business and politics. At first, he resisted the idea. It wasn't in his plan. But after prayer, reflection, and some nudging from colleagues, he accepted the role.

Right away, Novak set a new tone for the agency. On his first afternoon, sitting at the end of the long conference table in his office, he told his weary staff, "I'm the new sheriff in town, and it's going to be different with me." Then he met with each of his direct reports to find out what major issues they were concerned about, as well as the three or four projects they needed to accomplish. Novak's actions quickly signaled what the top priority was for him – building a mission-focused, people-focused culture.

His guiding principle was simple: "We are in the people business." He repeated this statement so often, it became a mantra within the agency. He wanted his entire staff to acknowledge that nothing happens without people and that good relationships were the fuel that motivated people to work hard for each other and ultimately do well together.

Novak's leadership style was visible even in small things. Where past directors had plastered their offices with plaques and photos of themselves with dignitaries, his office decor was quite different. He stripped away the "I love me" walls and replaced them with large scrolling digital photo displays of staff members, agency partners, and colleagues. These photos were a deliberate, daily reminder to everyone who came into the office that it was about "the people."

The most important decisions we make are about who we bring in.

He wasted no time addressing people mismatches across the agency. He identified key roles that would be filled differently from the TFC's prior practices. He used what he called a "bullseye" system. In the bullseye was someone he already knew and trusted. In the next ring was someone vouched for by a trusted contact. As the rings moved further from the center, the riskier the potential hire. This hiring approach significantly reduced hiring miscues and people mismatches. As Novak put it, "We're in the people business, so the most important decisions we make are about who we bring in."

Novak addressed team roles misalignments as quickly as they appeared. From his years of experience running his own companies, he knew his subordinate leaders needed to have healthy working relationships, and he addressed conflict head-on. Whenever he discovered his executive leaders were not communicating or were involved in one-upmanship behavior, he pulled them into the same room and made them work it out. Then, of course, the discussion would end in Novak reminding the leaders, "we're in the people business," and to be successful as an agency, the team (especially the executive leaders) had to work well together, break down silos, and talk to each other. "It wasn't always comfortable, but it built respect," Novak said.

He viewed leadership like he was conducting an orchestra. To make great music, the different sections – finance, operations, HR, construction – each had their roles, but it was his job to make sure they played in harmony.

Novak didn't just talk about compassion – he practiced servant leadership. He walked the walk and refused to ask anyone to do something he wouldn't do himself. As that spirit spread, employees began to trust again. The toxic culture gave way to one where people felt valued, they valued the roles and contributions of other departments, and executive leaders and managers began communicating more effectively and frequently with each other. The silo behavior across the agency was replaced by collaborative efforts.

From Failing to Thriving

The transformation of the Texas Facilities Commission is proof of what happens when compassionate, success-minded leaders build momentum. Stalled minor construction and building renovation projects were completed with excellence. When Novak took over, the agency had been labeled a failure, barely holding together with a $2 billion budget and no clear vision. Just a few years later, the budget had jumped to $6 billion. In 2020, TFC won the Engineering News-Record (ENR) Regional Best Projects Owner of the Year Award, as well as the NAFA Clean Air Award. Where the agency had once fought rats and aging facilities, it now showcased state-of-the-art new buildings that symbolized Texas pride.

TFC's fabulous success and turnaround also gave the executive director credibility. Novak's candor and willingness to make uncomfortable statements with lawmakers earned trust. In one memorable moment before the Senate Finance Committee, when asked about the troubled Hobby Building, he didn't sugarcoat. He told them bluntly, "That building's a piece of junk. It shouldn't even be in our portfolio." Instead of backlash, lawmakers applauded his honesty, with one lawmaker replying, "Finally, someone who gets it." That transparency was a stark contrast to the evasions of past leadership.

Take Every Opportunity to Give Without Expectation

Most striking of all, the Facilities Commission proved it could handle complex, high-stakes projects, including the Texas border wall program. One day, the governor called Novak into his office and tasked him to "build the Texas border wall" that would be state-funded. As Novak sat alone at the end of the long conference table in his office, he pondered how he and his staff of roughly 400-plus people could tackle this construction project that was previously accomplished by the U.S. Army Corps of Engineers - an organization of 37,000 civilian and military people. During his entrepreneurial career, he'd built buildings, aircraft hangars, and cell towers in South America, but never a contiguous 30-foot-high wall structure.

During the initial planning stages, Novak decided that this construction project far exceeded his agency's capability to manage the project. So his first step was to build a precision team – to hire professional experts in construction project management to augment the agency's legal, finance, and procurement teams. He also worked closely with sister state agencies such as the Texas Department of Public Safety, Texas Comptroller's Office, and the Texas Commission on Environmental Quality. There was close coordination with the governor's Texas Tactical Border Force and U.S. Border Patrol.

Once Novak's wall construction team was in place, they went to work. His coalition of military veterans, engineers, and contractors delivered results faster and cleaner than the U.S. Army Corps of Engineers had done – and on privately owned land - without asking the governor for one eminent domain authorization. No one can deny the competence, credibility, and momentum Novak's leadership created in completing this four-year, approximately 83-mile project.

TFC's transformation is proof of what happens when compassionate, success-minded leaders build momentum.

At the core of Novak's success is his insatiable appetite to invigorate transformational change. He is comfortable with being and doing the uncomfortable. Without question, Novak has continually taken every opportunity to give without expectation. Over his career, he has built many precision teams by tapping into his professional and personal network. Novak's "we're in the people business" attitude propels him to continually perform acts of generosity, producing an enormous ecosystem of trust. When Novak called colleagues and contacts for assistance with building the wall, they leaned in. That's how you build momentum!

The turnaround at the Texas Facilities Commission was dramatic: from a culture of dysfunctionality and distrust to one of high-performance, respect, and collaboration; from stalled major and minor construction projects with continual schedule slips and underwhelming tenant agency customer care to billion-dollar projects and award-winning facilities; from an agency others dismissed to one now viewed as indispensable.

Summary Takeaways

The Texas Facilities Commission's rebirth wasn't about buildings. It was about people. Mike Novak's story reminds us that achieving transformational change and unsurpassed organizational achievement requires compassionate leadership and momentum-building relationships.

CHAPTER 12

Compassionate Success Leadership – Maximizing Organizational Performance and Growth

"The Compassionate Success Mindset isn't just a concept. It's a choice – one you make every day."
– Kymberli Speight

Having a Compassionate Success Mindset is the Fundamental Building Block for Generating Momentum

Organizations that consistently perform well have a leader who understands the Compassionate Success Mindset. The U.S. Army gets it. Their motto, *"Mission First, People Always,"* clearly sends the message that ensuring America's national security is premier, but taking care of the soldiers who carry out this mission is equally important. The Navy's motto also recognizes the importance of taking care of the people who accomplish the mission in their motto, *"Ship, Shipmate, Self."* Mike Novak continually reminded his Facilities Commission team that "We are in the people business." Highly effective leaders in both the private and public sectors understand this fundamental axiom of consistent high performance.

Leaders with a big why, who aren't afraid to make tough decisions in uncomfortable moments and take every opportunity to give without expectation, possess the Compassionate Success Mindset. They expect the people they lead to treat others inside and outside the organization with respect (even when working through conflict).

When you have a leader who accepts, approves, appreciates, and respects others, it's easy to see where the Social Science Momentum Equation: $Ps = m |Vr|$ comes into play. Building momentum to take on a big project, resolve a long-standing problem, or move an organization's performance from poor to exceptional or good to great is only a person, a skill set, or key people away. Successful leaders turn to their professional and personal networks to help them when they need it. Whether they're seeking advice or collaboration, solving stagnant performance issues, or filling a skill set or knowledge gap, accomplishing their objective will depend on how large their "m" is and the quality "$|Vr|$" of those relationships.

CONCLUSION

If you've made it this far, something in these pages spoke to you – challenged you. The message in this book may have simply confirmed what you intuitively already knew. Maybe it lit a fire that's been dormant for a while. In any case, this book is a reminder and a tool for emerging and prospective leaders who want to lead a high-performance, best-in-class organization or team. I wrote this book for those leaders who want to grow their organization's performance from mediocre or miserably failing to high performing.

Whatever this book has stirred up, here's the point: without action on your part, it's just another book stating the obvious - people are the most important component of any strategy to accomplish a goal or objective. If you want to affect transformational change, with employees and teams achieving more than they ever thought possible, with positive, winning, upbeat attitudes, and having a strong, respected brand, it will take your deliberate investment in relational capital!

This is not a program or step-by-step method to implement top-down through your subordinate leaders. Taking action means making the daily decision to be aware of every person you meet with or who crosses your path. It's being comfortable with being uncomfortable and making tough decisions. It means making it your business to ensure your leaders are working well together and constructively and continually communicating with each other. It means ensuring your leaders are collaborating on solutions and recommendations for your approval and facilitating effective, candid conflict resolution. It's showing up with a mindset that says, "I see you. I believe in you. And I expect the best from you."

Mike Novak didn't rebuild the Texas Facilities Commission's brand and build 80-plus miles of border wall by talking about it. He did it by leading with a Compassionate Success Mindset and building an unstoppable surge of momentum through a massive investment in relational capital.

Fortunately, you have access to the most important ingredient in Novak's, or any great leader's, formula for success – people! This isn't a call for seeing everyone on your path as a delicious prime rib roast (or nut roast for vegetarians). This is a call for you to value people in your charge instead of using them. If you firmly grasp this concept, you'll have the opportunity to see how much more value they generate towards the team or organization's objectives. Leadership is about managing relationships toward a common objective that ends with success that is shared.

One Final Thought

Some of you will take these concepts seriously and begin incorporating them into your leadership regimen. Then, you'll set out to build momentum to help transform your organization, and you may experience limited to little success.

The logical conclusion will be either "I'm not doing enough" or that the Compassionate Success Mindset is overrated. Remember, the same forces of resistance in physics (inertia – the resistance to changes in motion, and friction – the action of surfaces rubbing against one another) are at work in the social science momentum equation also.

It's tough to overcome the inertia of a stuck or low-performing organization, one with people who have bad habits and attitudes, dysfunctional relationships, and low morale. There are also organizational friction forces - conflict, the clash of wills and temperaments, and, in some cases, hostility - all working against the momentum you're trying to build. It goes without saying that you will have to build enough momentum to overcome the forces of inertia and friction in your organization. This means you will need to expand your network of relationships, especially in the areas of knowledge, skillsets, and experiences your organization does not have.

You can do it! Transforming a failing agency with fired executives into an award-winning organization and being asked to take on a U.S. federal-level project is proof that it can be done! How did Novak do it? The answer is simple - by investing in "people."

To learn more, visit <u>Kymberlispeight.com</u> or scan the QR code below:

ACKNOWLEDGEMENTS

Many thanks to ...

My husband, Joel, for your love, vision, and continued support. You made this book possible.

Mike Novak, for generously sharing your story.

Neal and Lettie Maguire, for listening to my story and for your encouragement that this topic was valuable for leaders to hear.

Carl, for writing the foreword of this book, and for the many insights shared.

Jeff, Brian, Ezra, and Glenn, for taking the time to read and endorse this work.

All who opened a door that I was able to walk through.

ABOUT THE AUTHOR

Kymberli S. Speight is a dynamic leadership coach, keynote speaker, and consultant with over 20 years of executive experience. Having delivered more than 400 presentations and coached senior leaders worldwide, she specializes in helping organizations strengthen culture, trust, and performance through authentic relationship building.

Kymberli is the creator of the Compassionate Success framework — a philosophy that blends connection, empathy, and accountability to drive transformational results. Her engaging approach empowers executives and emerging leaders alike to unlock their potential, build thriving teams, and sustain meaningful momentum.

Known for her signature travel jacket embroidered with the words "Connections Matter," Kymberli embodies her message wherever she goes — reminding others that success is never achieved alone. She and her husband, Joel, live their lives committed to helping others rediscover the power of genuine human connection.

APPENDIX: REFERENCES

1. American Management Association, "Leading Turnarounds: Avoiding Early Mistakes" (2025), https://www.amanet.org/articles/leading-turnarounds-avoiding-early-mistakes/

2. Southern Management Association, Sage Journals, https://www.amanet.org/articles/leading-turnarounds-avoiding-early-mistakes/

3. University of Pretoria, "Understanding Turnaround Leadership in Business" (2019), https://repository.up.ac.za/server/api/core/bitstreams/3a55bb73-1f79-4301-ba1a-d6f97dacf20d/content

4. Deloitte, "Turnaround Strategies for Dysfunctional Teams" (2016) https://www.deloitte.com/us/en/insights/topics/leadership/dysfunctional-teams-turnaround-strategies-team-performance.html

5. Home Furnishings Association, "7 Common Leadership Mistakes and How to Fix Them" (2025), https://myhfa.org/7-common-leadership-mistakes-and-how-to-fix-them/

6. National College of Ireland, "Turnaround Management: An Explorative Investigation of the Strategic Leadership Competencies for the Turnaround of Indian IT Firms" (2019), https://norma.ncirl.ie/3992/1/ashleyrajivmathad.pdf

7. Work Institute, 2024 Retention Report, https://info.workinstitute.com/hubfs/2024%20Retention%20Report/Work%20Institute%202024%20Retention%20Report.pdf

8. Aknin, Dunn, Norton, & colleagues ("Impact Unlocks the Emotional Benefits of Prosocial Spending," 2013) https://dash.harvard.edu/server/api/core/bitstreams/7312037c-f764-6bd4-e053-0100007fdf3b/content

9. Grant & Dutton, "Beneficiary or Benefactor: "Are People More Prosocial When They Reflect on Receiving or Giving?" (2012), https://faculty.wharton.upenn.edu/wp-content/uploads/2013/04/GrantDutton_PsychScience2012.pdf

10. Hui et al., "Rewards of Kindness? A Meta-Analysis of the Link Between Prosociality and Well-Being" (2020), https://pubmed.ncbi.nlm.nih.gov/32881540/

11. Chancellor et al. "Everyday Prosociality in the Workplace: The Reinforcing Benefits of Giving, Getting, and Glimpsing." (2018), https://pubmed.ncbi.nlm.nih.gov/28581323/

12. Aaker, Norton, Rudd, "Getting the Most Out of Giving: Concretely Framing a Prosocial Goal Maximizes Happiness" (2014), https://www.hbs.edu/ris/Publication%20Files/Getting%20The%20Most%20Out%20of%20Giving_8b7bb2dd-7187-4a46-a521-479e1a7eb671.pdf

13. Wikipedia, Referral Economy (2025)

14. The New York Times, "7 Surprising Stats about Customer Referral Programs" (2013)

15. Minsky, Quesenberry, Harvard Business Review, "How B2B Sales Can Benefit from Social Selling" (2016), https://hbr.org/2016/11/84-of-b2b-sales-start-with-a-referral-not-a-salesperson

16. Gallup, "42% of Employee Turnover Is Preventable but Often Ignored" (2024), https://www.gallup.com/workplace/646538/employee-turnover-preventable-often-ignored.aspx

17. Taylor-Chadwick, "Employee Retention Statistics: Key Stats Every Manager Should Know (2024), Runn.io/blog/employee-retention-statistics